About Demos

Demos is a greenhouse for new ideas which can improve the quality of our lives. As an independent think tank, we aim to create an open resource of knowledge and learning that operates beyond traditional party politics.

We connect researchers, thinkers and practitioners to an international network of people changing politics. Our ideas regularly influence government policy, but we also work with companies, NGOs, colleges and professional bodies.

Demos knowledge is organised around five themes, which combine to create new perspectives. The themes are democracy, learning, enterprise, quality of life and global change.

But we also understand that thinking by itself is not enough. Demos has helped to initiate a number of practical projects which are delivering real social benefit through the redesign of public services.

We bring together people from a wide range of backgrounds to cross-fertilise ideas and experience. By working with Demos, our partners develop a sharper insight into the way ideas shape society. For Demos, the process is as important as the final product.

www.demos.co.uk

First published in 2004
© Demos
Some rights reserved – see copyright licence for details

ISBN 1 84180 128 3
Typeset by Land & Unwin, Bugbrooke
Printed by Hendy Banks, London

For further information and
subscription details please contact:

Demos
Magdalen House
136 Tooley Street
London SE1 2TU

telephone: 0845 458 5949
email: hello@demos.co.uk
web: www.demos.co.uk

Home Alone

Combating isolation with older housebound people

Helen McCarthy
Gillian Thomas

DEM☺S

Contents

Executive summary

1. The risk of loneliness is increasing. Altered family structures, geographical mobility and longevity are all contributing factors to greater levels of loneliness in hidden segments of society. Knowing how to combat loneliness is not straightforward. Many of these risk factors are actually associated with aspects of social progress that we cherish such as greater personal choice and freedom. Yet, as a society, we should not tolerate loneliness for the minority simply as the price we pay for the social advances enjoyed by the majority.

2. Government has taken a great number of measures to protect those most at risk of loneliness and isolation: the elderly and housebound. The 2001 *National Service Framework for Older People* outlined new principles, which aim to ensure that services fit round the individual rather than around professional provider roles.[1] The 1999 Royal Commission on Long Term Care recommended a whole host of measures, including more domiciliary services, to help promote older people's independence.[2]

3. This appears to be the right strategy, yet the evidence suggests it is not doing enough to prevent loneliness and isolation in old age: 32 people die alone and unnoticed in their own homes each year; one in six older people living alone rate themselves

as 'often or always lonely' and this number is increasing. Demos has calculated that unless significant changes occur, by 2021 nearly 2.2 million of over-65s will be socially isolated.[3] So just what is going wrong?

4. The answer lies in the failure of government to grasp that the key to reducing loneliness lies not with the state, or even voluntary organisations and community groups, but with lonely people themselves. This realisation shifts the entire framework in which older people's services are offered. From this new perspective, the responsibility of providers is not simply to deliver services that meet people's physical or material needs, as assessed by professionals. Instead, it is about involving and supporting service users in 'co-producing' their own outcomes, so as to overcome loneliness in ways that they define for themselves. Unleashing 'co-production' through increasing the participation of older people will ultimately move the system towards greater personalisation in all aspects of service delivery.

5. The failure of policy to grasp fully this prospect explains why the current approach to combating isolation among older housebound people isn't working as well as it could or should. Services such as day and homecare focus too much on defining needs in narrowly technocratic terms, neglecting more promising pathways towards prevention and participation as a result. For many older housebound people, this approach undermines their sense of identity and self-esteem, with the only tolerable option being to reject services and offers of assistance entirely.

6. In fact, the services that are *most* likely fully to engage older housebound people are also the services that are most likely to suffer from budget squeeze at a local level. For example, the Women's Royal Voluntary Service (WRVS) runs a 'Home from Hospital' service, which brings volunteers and older people together so that they can work out the best strategies for

independent living after a spell in hospital. Yet because this service depends on local authority contracts it operates for a very limited time span, and in a limited geographical area. Other services such as book clubs and befriending schemes are very successful at motivating older housebound people, but they are often regarded as 'nice to have', rather than essential from a statutory perspective.

7.   Much procurement and commissioning of care and other related services is driven by the desire for 'best value'. Yet, in reality, using this criterion can lead to *reinforced isolation*. For example, many local authorities have moved from delivering a hot meal to isolated housebound people once a day to delivering them several frozen meals once a fortnight. This potentially delivers more choice to the user and achieves greater efficiency, but it reduces the precious social contact associated with daily delivery.

8.   The 'business' case for preventing or reducing social isolation should be obvious. The medical bill alone includes treatment arising from falls and fractures, depression and poor immunity to disease. Of course, some of this is caused by inevitable frailty in older age. But too often these health complaints are the direct result of isolated people living unsupported and demotivating lives. 'Delayed discharge' costs the NHS an estimated £170 million and 1.7 million lost bed days each year. The National Audit Office recently estimated that around 4,100 older patients on any given day are fit enough to leave hospital, but have nowhere appropriate to go.[4]

9.   Furthermore, the social costs of loneliness also loom large. Isolated people who lack opportunities to contribute to community life represent a huge resource of untapped potential. Friends and relatives are affected, too, and worry about how to ask for help, or how to cope.

10. This picture is bleak. Yet there are examples of good practice, particularly in the voluntary and community sector (VCS), where capacities for innovation and context-sensitive responses make co-production a palpable reality for older people. For example, some organisations offer peer mentoring programmes, which promote learning or exercise. Another example is the volunteering opportunities offered to older people, including those who are housebound, by a wide range of organisations like WRVS or the Retired and Senior Volunteer Programme, which forms part of Community Service Volunteers (CSV).

11. Too often these sorts of programmes and initiatives are unable to flourish or be rolled out more widely because of the constraints on statutory bodies with responsibility for commissioning and procuring care services from the VCS. Many VCS organisations have become core service providers and are forced to compete on grounds of efficiency and cost-effectiveness, even though they may create other types of value that cannot be easily captured using present indicators.

12. If the fight against loneliness and isolation is to be led by older housebound people themselves, policy needs to find ways of better supporting those people as co-producers. Changing the 'script' by which services are delivered and outcomes created will require policymakers and VCS providers to reconfigure the relationships that exist between formal services, home and community by putting users at the centre. This will inevitably have an impact on how services are commissioned, contracted, designed and delivered, and is a task for the longer rather than shorter term. Some useful first steps, however, might involve the following:

   O the criterion for commissioning social care for older housebound people to include indicators of 'co-production'

- community centres serving older housebound people in each of the top ten per cent most disadvantaged wards
- mainstreaming age into regeneration policy and delivery
- government review of community transport provision in the UK
- home from hospital mentors
- social exclusion unit taskforce
- boost for housebound friendly businesses
- promotion of volunteering to over-65s.

1. Introduction

Perhaps the greatest human fear is fear of loneliness. It takes an exceptional individual to hold no qualms at all about the absence of companionship, family and community in their life. Most of us are not so self-sufficient. Children bawl their eyes out when they are left alone. Young singles worry if they'll ever find that special someone with whom to share their lives. Parents worry what they'll do when the kids have flown the nest. But perhaps most of all we fear being lonely when we are old. We hope it won't happen to us, that we will stay healthy and supported by our families and friends; that we will have strong roots in our local communities with plenty of places to go and people to see; and that society will actively support our choices and structure itself in ways that include rather than exclude.

We all wish this for ourselves. And some of us will be fortunate and enjoy exactly these sorts of freedoms. And yet, in the last few decades, our lives have been changing in ways that actively *increase* our chances of becoming lonely in later life. For example, rates of childlessness and divorce are rising; there are more single-person households than ever before; geographical mobility makes it less likely that we'll live near members of our extended family; and longer life expectancy means that the odds of our becoming disabled in old age are growing. The principles of convenience, choice and accessibility shape our consumer culture, yet can end up having the exact opposite effect as we grow older and our needs change.

There are resilience factors too. Transformations in ICTs over the past decade have opened up the possibilities for staying in touch with loved ones and making new friends. Keeping physically active and getting involved in the neighbouring community through volunteering, local groups and other forms of civic participation are proven to extend years of active life and life satisfaction among older people.

Yet these bulwarks against loneliness and isolation are not readily available to all, and many older people remain housebound and invisible, dependent on services that too often meet neither their physical nor emotional needs. There is a strong case, on both moral and harder 'business' grounds, for policy to embrace an anti-loneliness agenda, in the same way that it has with child poverty or inequality on the basis of gender, race and disability.

This will require a rethinking of the way in which services are delivered and, indeed, the way the public realm is governed. The focus of this report is on that final destination, where few of us wish ourselves or others to be in later life: housebound, isolated and unsupported. Sadly, this is not a case of looking at the extreme experience of a tiny minority. The current population of over-65s is 9,576,000. The ESRC Growing Older Programme found that 17 per cent of over-65s in the UK are socially isolated (not in weekly contact with friends, family or neighbours).[5] We can conclude from this that there are 1,627,920 socially isolated over-65s in the UK. Using information from the Government Actuary Department, the projected population of those aged 65 and over in 2021 will be 12,736,000. If social isolation continues at its current rate (17 per cent of over-65s) we can conclude that 2,165,120 people of this age group will be socially isolated. This represents an increase of 33 per cent of socially isolated older people in the UK. The true figure could be even higher because of the under-reporting that characterises social isolation studies, and also because the risk factors for isolation are increasing.

Connections and disconnections

We are witnessing in our society a growing divide between the 'network-rich' and 'network-poor'. Technological advances have put millions of citizens, consumers and workers online, giving them unprecedented levels of access to information and new opportunities for social participation and cultural consumption. The last 20 years have seen increasing international flows of goods, people, ideas and money, driven by the processes of globalisation that characterise the world around us. It has prompted one eminent sociologist to herald this the age of the 'network society'.[6]

But as new links are forged, old ones are lost. Robert Putnam's 'bowling alone' thesis, with its in-depth analysis of the decline of civic trust in America over the past 30 years, has become the set text for appraising the impact of these global forces on the fabric of our community life.[7] This story in Britain has taken a distinctive path, with overall levels of so-called 'social capital' (a term relating to social networks, shared norms, values and understandings) holding up over the same period, but not evenly distributed across all socioeconomic groups. One prominent social scientist describes it thus: 'In fact, Britain is divided between a well-connected and active group of citizens with generally prosperous lives and another set whose associational life and involvement in politics is very limited.'[8]

Who then is at risk of social isolation in Britain today? Defining this condition is not an easy job. The ESRC Growing Older programme discusses social isolation in relation to 'the integration of individuals (and groups) into the wider social environment'.[9] It is usually measured by the size of one's social network – by the number, type and duration of contacts between individuals and the wider community.[10] Few of us analyse our circle of family members, friends, colleagues and acquaintances in quite this way. Yet it is exactly the nature of that web of connection in which we live that shapes our chances of being isolated in later life.

What makes this picture more complex is that many identifiable 'risk factors' reflect aspects of social change that have, taken together, improved our quality of life and increased our personal freedoms. For example, the rise in single-person households (up by 26 per cent between 1991 and 2001[11]) is linked to the increasing instability of household composition, as people live longer and experience more periods of living independently, either before relationship formation or after relationships are ended by divorce, separation or death. The divorce rate has been steadily climbing since the 1950s, peaking at 180,000 a year in 1993 and settling at 157,000 by 2001. The proportion of older people represented in this figure has also been on the rise, with one projection putting it at 13 per cent by 2021.[12]

Living alone may represent freedom and independence for younger people, but it becomes a palpable risk factor for isolation with age. Reported levels of loneliness among older people are higher among those who live alone compared with those who live with others: 17 per cent of older people living alone rate themselves as 'often or always lonely', compared with two per cent of those who live with others, and 80 per cent of the 'often lonely' category live alone.[13]

Another trend is towards greater opportunity for mobility, leading to families becoming more geographically dispersed.[14] Inter-generational households are now very rare; only a very small proportion of children over the age of 35 live with their parents, and just five per cent of over-65s live with an adult child.[15] This affects the frequency of contact between family members and makes the prospect of having one's nearest and dearest at hand in later life a distant one. For example, 88 per cent of those who live within a 30-minute journey of a non-resident mother see her at least once a week, compared with only 13 per cent of those who live further away.[16]

With more women of working age entering the labour market there has been a further alteration of the dynamics of individuals' social networks, as women have traditionally borne primary responsibility for maintaining family ties across generations. Many women continue to provide this role, and they are still more likely than men to see parents, grown-up children and other relatives regularly.[17] Nonetheless, the squeeze on their time is getting ever tighter, as growing interest in the 'work-life balance' agenda aptly demonstrates.

These trends have profound implications for mapping social connectivity in Britain today, and help us to identify where the fault lines of the network society run deepest. Social networks display a 'poor get poorer' property. That is, those with little contact with family tend to have fewer friends, too, as these two types of network reinforce each other, and the more friends a person has the more likely they are to belong to an organisation and the more likely they are to participate in its activities.[18] According to one study, among those with more than 19 close friends, over a third belong to two or more organisations – more than double the rate of those with fewer than four.[19]

This may not feel like such a big deal when you are young, non-disabled and in employment. But friends become a scarcer commodity with age, as contemporaries move away and the prospect of limited physical mobility reduces the scope for meeting new people. According to one study, the percentage of people who believe they have ten or more close friends goes down with age, partly as a result of the increasing death rate among any given individual's cohort of friends. This figure peaks at 58 per cent in the 34 to 45 age group before falling to 39 per cent among over-65s.[20]

Gerontologist GC Wenger argues that, for older people, this is the moment when the quality of one's 'support network' becomes crucial to well-being. Wenger describes this as 'that core of the larger social network whose members are available – or perceived to be available – to provide emotional support or companionship, instrumental help, advice and information as needed on a day-to-day basis'.[21] In other words, it's only when the risk of isolation looms largest that you find out who your real friends are.

Institutions and individuals

So old age itself is inevitably a risk factor for isolation. In fact, 17 per cent of over-65s in the UK could be classified as socially isolated, and today there are fewer older people reporting themselves to be 'never lonely' than in previous decades.[22] Some of the risk factors that contribute to social isolation identified by social scientists are listed in the box below. These risk factors are most pertinent to the generation approaching older age, and possibly experiencing some forms of isolation already. We argue the risks to younger people of becoming isolated in 40 or 50 years time are also stark, but are less well documented. For the 'friends generation', having a social network that is geographically disparate and spending long periods of time outside close family relationships is the norm. Yet these are known risk factors for isolation in later life. Loneliness for this generation is likely to be all the more devastating because of their high expectations of social networks.

Many of the risk factors for isolation, particularly around marital status and family situation, are part of the string of accidents, opportunities, random acts and unforeseen events that constitute a typical life. They cannot necessarily be accounted for, and nor in a free society would we wish them to be. As history has shown, social policy is unlikely to be successful in reversing risk factors by attacking divorce or high geographical mobility.

The key to overcoming loneliness is in nurturing the 'resilience' factors that can combat both the causes and symptoms of loneliness. Individuals themselves can act by ensuring they have the ability to make new friends as their circumstances change, having the 'know-how' to access information on services, and through lifelong commitment to volunteering. The responsibility for nurturing resilience does not lie entirely with the individual. Institutions and social policy could and should act in ways that reduce the likelihood of social isolation, and help to treat the symptoms where they are already present.

Risk and resilience factors for social isolation in later life

Risk:

- O childlessness or having children that live far away
- O divorce or separation
- O living alone
- O having or developing a physical or mental impairment
- O living in a rural area
- O small and homogeneous social network.

Resilience:
- O   having children who live nearby
- O   marriage or remarriage or long-term partner
- O   living with a partner or family
- O   having a large and diverse circle of friends
- O   regular exercise and physical activity
- O   membership of local organisations, groups and clubs
- O   access to ICTs and skills to use them.

This is not only part of a social justice agenda; there are compelling reasons why government and other agencies should act in order to secure the modernisation and long-term sustainability of our public services and to promote social cohesion more broadly. There is some evidence that government already recognises the pressures on the informal care economy which keeps children safe and older people supported. Parents with young or disabled children enjoy some flexible working rights, and in April 2004 Tony Blair announced his intention to extend these to workers caring for elderly parents too.[23]

This 'time liberation' dilemma will continue to occupy a space at the heart of the social isolation agenda for many years to come. Yet the needs of carers are only part of the story. Arguably the most important dimension of institutional reform concerns the quality of specialist care delivered to older people, and its relationship to the universal services that we all need and use. Domiciliary or homecare services are crucial for supporting older people to live independently in their homes, and day care centres and programmes provide a vital link to the wider community. Within mainstream services, public transport, particularly local bus networks, provide a lifeline for many older people. Initiatives to widen access to ICTs offer opportunities for older people to stay in touch with family and friends and discover a wide range of learning resources.

Many of these services involve voluntary sector providers who see their core mission in terms of fighting social isolation and building inclusive communities. As well as delivering formally contracted services, many charities such as Age Concern, Help the Aged and WRVS engage in additional projects and initiatives aimed at alleviating isolation, from community transport schemes and befriending programmes to lunch clubs and group excursions.

Supporting choices

This array of public services, social activities and civic participation represent a potential bedrock of inclusion that wards off the likelihood of isolation for those able to access and make the most of it. Yet it is not simply a question of making these opportunities available and then sitting back and watching the incidence of isolation disappear from a neighbourhood or community. Genuine inclusion requires hard work sustained over time.

This is because the relationship between isolation and loneliness is not straightforward, and for many older people who have previously lived lives of independence and autonomy the emotional dimensions can be even greater. First, we must recognise that even those who have little contact with others may be exercising an active choice. It is, in fact, possible to be technically 'isolated' as measured by social scientists, but not 'lonely' – as loneliness is an evaluation made by individuals on their own level and quality of social contact and engagement.

It is important, in particular for service providers, not to prejudge the choices of older people who live alone, as one historian of old age argues: 'The statistics show more older people living alone, but it does not mean that they are necessarily lonely and isolated from friends and family, though this is certainly true of some; they also show more people exercising the choice to live their own lives, unconstrained by having to share with their families.'[24]

Furthermore, appreciating the complexity of loneliness can be a tall order. For most, loneliness is experienced over a period of time. It is never entirely static, and its intensity can increase or decrease, especially if triggered by a change in circumstances such as a period of ill health. Alternatively, for some, loneliness is associated with certain times of the day, for instance evenings at home alone, or it could be an ongoing experience characterising all aspects of daily life.

Most people inevitably experience at least one of these types of loneliness at some time in their lives, regardless of age and whether they live alone or with others. Yet the assessment of loneliness among older people has largely been dominated by quantitative methods, which can fail to capture the complexity of individuals' experiences of loneliness. Qualitative studies suggest that participants in surveys of this kind may under-report the extent of their loneliness, regarding it as something bearing a social stigma, or wanting to 'put a brave face on things'.[25] Certainly few of us wish to think of ourselves as lonely people, and there's no reason to believe older people living on their own feel any differently.

This can create a dilemma for service providers, who do not want to make assumptions about an individual's level of loneliness, but at the same time wish to provide (and in many cases are obliged statutorily to provide) support where genuine need exists. The problem is that in this field that need is rarely transparent. Inevitably, it is as complex and multifaceted as the individual it is attached to. Complex needs require complex solutions. They also require 'adaptive' capacity among providers from all sectors, of the kind that enables them to reconfigure their offering so as to provide genuinely personalised services.[26]

The rise of the demanding 'consumer' of public services has, in recent years, been central to most diagnoses of the challenge of modernisation, with extending choice held as a general panacea. The limitations of this approach are now beginning to become apparent. American academic Barry Schwarz, for example, has persuasively argued that the psychological stresses of choosing from an increasing number of competing offers often pushes people back towards the judgements of 'experts' rather than taking the decisions for themselves.[27]

The realisation that too much choice can be debilitating has created a space for a new vision of 'personalisation' to emerge as a principle for public services reform. This is founded on the ability of users not only to access the services they need, but also to play an active role in the design and delivery of those services. This creates more responsive services, as well as legitimacy and hence public value.

Personalising services to the housebound

Personalisation, as we will see in Chapter 3, holds out much hope for older housebound people, whose complex needs and desire for independent lives, perhaps more than any other group, must be actively valued, legitimated and supported by society, and positively enabled by institutions that deliver crucial services, both to the home and to the community. The 'consumer' model is particularly limited in the context of this group, for it is those very principles of choice, convenience and accessibility when applied inappropriately that represent some of the most serious forces for isolation, as has been the case, for example, with some Meals on Wheels services (see Chapter 3).

To make personalisation a reality the needs of older housebound people will need to be considered explicitly and brought into mainstream policy from the obvious areas of health and social care, and included in wider strategies for public transport, e-government, regeneration and anti-poverty. Yet the vision of personalisation means more than disaggregating need by age group. It means getting seriously personal in the way services and users come together to create joint outcomes.

One study from the ESRC's Growing Older Programme describes the inner conflicts experienced by some older people between 'the need to sustain one's identity and self-worth and the acceptance of help and services'.[28] Dependency on others for support directly challenges the sense of identity and self-esteem that each individual builds up over a whole lifetime. In this light, it is often more important to an older person to protect these than to adjust to 'appropriate' or 'convenient' solutions to the needs of later life as offered by service providers.[29]

The experience of limited mobility makes this sort of 'identity work' particularly challenging for an older housebound person. Providers too struggle to design and deliver services in ways that are sensitive to the complexity of identity and need in all its forms. One route to personalisation is through 'co-production', an approach to service design that encourages providers and users to see themselves in a new context, with bottom-up solutions that create the public good as the ultimate goal. As Charles Leadbeater argues, the objective of providers is 'to build up the knowledge and confidence of the users to take action themselves', and that of the users is to become 'active participants in the process' and 'co-producers' of their own health, education or care.

Personalising services for the housebound will require transforming the way we think – even the way we speak – about the relationship between provider and user, and breaking down the category of dependency that so damages older people's quality of life. It will also require taking another look at the way we approach wider community issues, social cohesion and participation. Isolation affects individuals where they are not integrated with the wider social environment, and policies and initiatives aimed at 'inclusion' must find imaginative and new ways of linking home and community. For the housebound, this objective is crucial if being 'at home' is to mean being at the heart of one's community, and not on its margins.

This report attempts to open this conversation by setting out in detail the reality of being older and housebound in the UK today, and building a picture of an alternative world in which individuals' choices are fully supported by innovative and personalised service delivery. It is structured as follows. Chapter 2 explores the experience of older housebound people in greater depth, and makes the case for government and other stakeholders to take action to close the gaps in current provision. Chapter 3 reviews the policy context, exploring the limitations of current commitments to engaging service users, and assessing the potential of a new approach, characterised by personalised, co-produced services for improving older housebound people's quality of life. Chapter 4 draws on new research perspectives and innovative practice currently being pioneered in the UK as a way of demonstrating how the 'script' for delivering services to those at risk of isolation *can* be changed. In Chapter 5 we draw our conclusions and make recommendations aimed at a range of stakeholders for transforming services to Britain's hidden housebound, and bringing their experiences, hopes and aspirations out of the front door.

2. Being Home Alone

Summary

Sustaining continuity in terms of home, personal relationships and social activities is central to well-being for older people. Yet policy and provision have not worked hard enough to support older housebound people in living independent lives, viewing them primarily as a technical category of need. The case for transforming services to older housebound people needs to be articulated more strongly. This involves recognising not only the moral case for treating everyone with dignity and respect, but also the pay-offs in terms of modernising Britain's public services and enlarging the potential contribution of older people to their families, neighbours and wider community.

We spend a great portion of our lives in our homes, sleeping, eating, watching television, reading books, doing the housework or entertaining guests. Britain is a house-proud nation, as reflected in our TV schedules that are fit to bursting with home-centred shows. The home is the private space that we are free to make our own, and where we are free to come and go as we please. It is also the primary site where family relationships are formed and caring takes place.

However, not everyone has such an easy relationship with where they live. For some, as their needs change over time, home becomes a space that is difficult to manage, that no longer fits their physical requirements, and even begins to take on the characteristics of a prison as the world outside recedes. Becoming housebound in this way attacks an individual's very self-esteem and confidence, as they struggle to adjust to their new limitations in a space that once met their needs and was their pride and joy.[30]

Yet the common solution that society offers is not an appealing one either. Residential or nursing care, for all the dedicated individuals who work in that sector, is seen by many older or disabled people as the final resort, and something to be resisted for as long as possible.[31] Many see entering a care home as confirmation that they are physically and mentally on a 'downward spiral', as the likelihood of this occurrence increases with old age.

Social isolation affects many groups, but it takes on a particularly acute form for those with seriously limited mobility outside their homes. The very word 'housebound' has negative connotations, conjuring up images of helplessness and dependence. And yet this word, used most commonly by social services departments to assess a certain category of need, captures an important aspect of social isolation for many older people, which deserves to be treated separately from more general discussion of isolation and exclusion. A MORI survey of 2000 found that 12 per cent of people aged 65 and over feel trapped in their own home.[32] And a government survey from 1998, asking respondents how they would feel if they had to spend a week in their house without visitors or being able to go out, found that 53 per cent would be really bored, 47 per cent would be lonely, and 20 per cent would get claustrophobic.[33]

In other words, although most older people would prefer to stay in their own homes than enter residential care, they do not necessarily want to spend every waking hour in them. One study found that common strategies for coping with loneliness include sitting in car parks or going to the library and shops simply to be among other people.[34] Yet for housebound people even this is not an option. Their material reality consists of the four walls around them. The immediate built environment in which they spend the majority of their time is, quite possibly, the most relevant fact of their isolation. In this light, 'housebound' is as meaningful a category for thinking about disadvantage and exclusion as other more familiar categories of analysis such as disability, race, ethnicity, gender, socioeconomic status and even age. And yet, as we will see, there is nothing inevitable about the link between limited mobility and social isolation. Breaking that connection should be prioritised and made explicit as a public policy goal.

Identifying the housebound

So exactly who is housebound in Britain today? This is not a widely used category for analysing social disadvantage, deployed primarily by social work practitioners as a technical category for assessing needs and entitlements for services such as home helps or Meals on Wheels. Yet, taking a wider view, the housebound are members of a complex group taking in both old age and disability (which are categories that often overlap, as the likelihood of becoming disabled increases with age), as well as a range of other risk factors. For example, other groups at risk of becoming housebound include lone parents, sufferers of domestic violence and some ethnic minorities, especially where living in an area of deprivation and high crime or where cultural norms prevent women from travelling unaccompanied much beyond the limits of their immediate neighbourhood (see Figure 1).

Figure 1: Categories of housebound people

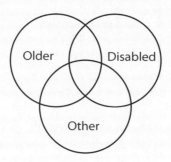

For the purposes of this report we define the 'housebound' as those living alone in their own homes *without the support system they desire in place*, and we focus on older people, as they represent a large proportion of this group and are particularly at risk. For example, the number of older people living alone in Britain is extremely high compared with other countries: 15 per cent of one-person households in Britain involve a householder aged 65 or older, compared with 11.8 per cent in France and 7.5 per cent in Spain. In fact, Britain is only topped by Denmark, where the figure is 17.5 per cent.[35]

Table 1 shows the number of people aged 65 and over living alone in the UK in 2004. The high number of women in this group is the result of high rates of widowhood. This is still the norm for older women: nearly half of women aged 65 and over are widowed in the UK, rising to four-fifths of the over-85s (although the gender gap in life expectancy is closing).[36] Divorce is creating more single households among the over-65s, too. The percentage of older people who are divorced rose from one per cent to five per cent between 1971 and 2001, and the Office for National Statistics estimates that this will reach more than 13 per cent by 2021.[37]

Table 1: People aged 65 and over living alone in the UK in 2004

Age	Percentage living alone	Total in that age bracket (000)
Males 65–74	17.5	2,045
Males 75–84	25.7	1,168
Males 85 and over	36.9	281
All males over 65	21.8	3,494
Females 65–74	33.2	2,322
Females 75–84	52.5	1,765
Females 85 and over	54.5	732
All females 65 and over	43.5	4,819

Source: ONS, *Social Trends* 34 (2004)

Just as living alone does not equate with being housebound, being older and living alone does not equate with it either. Yet the combination of age and single-householder status, as we have already seen, is a recognised risk factor. Marital status and living arrangements are pivotal to an older person's financial well-being, social relationships and access to carers should they become frail or disabled. Furthermore, the risk of losing one's physical mobility increases in old age. According to the 2001 Census, more than half (52.8 per cent) of pensioners living alone have a limiting long-term illness.[38]

The case for tackling social isolation

Social invisibility is a defining feature of the experience of isolation. For this reason the extent of this phenomenon often only becomes apparent through depressing statistics about the costs of 'bed-blocking' to the NHS, or shocking news stories about older people found dead in their homes after seeing no one for weeks on end. These manifestations of social isolation may make the headlines from time to time but, almost incredibly, they have failed to date to mobilise political action or inaugurate sustained and targeted change.

The reasons for this are grimly predictable. First, people in government have a silo mentality about older people, whose needs often fall down the crack between health and social care. Secondly, and perhaps most crucially, as a society we lack the imagination to envisage viable long-term alternatives to residential care and the will to put them into action. This is despite a growing consensus around the unintended damaging effects of large-scale, institutionalised settings for mental health services and services for children in care, and the move towards smaller units or home-based care for these individuals. As ageing specialists Arber and Ginn argue, 'entering a residential or nursing home is usually considered a major threat to autonomy which older people resist until there is no alternative'.[39] The salient question, then, is who decides when there is no alternative and how.

What is required is a shot in the arm to get policymakers and practitioners thinking about alternative futures in a sustained and strategic manner. The first step is to be clear about why this is a priority for policy. The case for keeping people at home for longer should be overwhelming. This is not only from the moral perspective of the basic human right to be treated with dignity and respect, but also from a pragmatic assessment of the challenges of modernisation facing British public institutions. This case has not been made powerfully or nearly often enough. The remainder of this chapter, therefore, spells out and elaborates this case, point by point.

Point 1: Independent living can and should be an option for the many

There is often an assumption among both families and care professionals that there comes a point when an older person can no longer survive on his or her own, and that full-time residential care is the only way to ensure their physical health and safety or to prevent isolation.

For many, this may be true. Yet, as the disability movement has taught us, 'living independently' need not mean total self-sufficiency. We are all dependent on others for our health and well-being to some extent, and some individuals are further along that spectrum than others. One's position on that spectrum, however, should not determine the level of control one has over one's life.

Disabled people of all ages often see independence in terms of making active decisions and having their own voice, rather than physically doing everything for themselves.[40] This appears to be the attitude of many older housebound people, too, as one study found: 'People's explanations of how they coped with disability tended to be couched in terms of inner emotional and intellectual resources followed by support from a family member.'[41] For many people who have developed an impairment in older age, the transition from one end of the spectrum towards the other is often traumatic. This means that many older housebound people see accepting services as an admission of defeat, or a sign of weakness of spirit or resolve. The same study found that the attitude of some older people towards their disability was close to denial.

However, if independent living were to become more publicly valued and supported as a viable choice for older people – even the very frail – such denial or ambivalence around accessing services would probably evaporate. Furthermore, technological advances are transforming the possibilities for keeping people living independently yet supported and safe. Wireless technologies hold out particular promise for remote or self-monitoring, and video telephony can connect patients to their GPs in entirely new ways.[42] Yet, generally, providers have not made full use of the technologies available to assist older people with high support needs in the home, which in most cases remain at the pilot stage and out of the reach of most housebound people in the UK today.

Point 2: Older people's needs must be mainstreamed on grounds of equity

'Citizen-centred services' is an article of faith for most policymakers and service providers in the UK. These stakeholders increasingly recognise the challenge of diversity for delivering responsive and appropriate services as well as protecting the principle of universal access. 'Mainstreaming' the needs of specific groups has been one route towards responsiveness and equity in service delivery, and has an important role to play in moving the system towards personalisation. This approach has seen significant progress in the case of understanding better the needs of ethnic minorities and women as service users. In fact, public bodies now have a 'positive duty' to promote race equality in all their activities, and this is soon to be extended to disability and gender.

The needs of older people, in comparison, have been neglected and in some cases older people have been actively discriminated against. This is despite evidence to suggest that where services are designed and delivered in appropriate ways, older people are able to engage with them positively without losing their self-esteem or independence. One study found that, when asked, older people said they wanted: 'practical, flexible, and low-level assistance that helps them to remain independent, gain the confidence to identify their own solutions and supports them in retaining their own social networks'.[43] It doesn't sound like a lot to ask, and yet so much of the world outside the home is not structured in ways that support the choices of older housebound people. For example, a significant minority of older people living in deprived areas feel that post offices, health and social care or welfare services and local transport services are missing from their neighbourhood.[44] A recent report by the Local Government Association concluded thus: 'Older people are often still excluded from universal services in the community – ones that we would all expect to use.'[45]

EU law requires the UK to outlaw age discrimination in employment and vocational employment from October 2006. Campaigning groups have argued that this should be extended to cover the provision of goods, facilities and services, and urged the government to consider extending the 'positive duty' to include age.[46] The evidence suggests that action of some sort is urgently required. One survey found that train and bus operators think of older people as a nuisance or as potentially reducing profits,[47] and age-based rationing still goes on in many hospitals and GP surgeries.[48] Negative images of older people abound, presenting them as a burdensome drain on public resources rather than legitimate users of services for all. Whether or not legislation is forthcoming, older people's right to be treated fairly and with respect must be championed now and into the future. This is not simply a moral issue, but a priority for ensuring the sustainability of our public services, as the next section spells out.

Point 3: Investing in preventing isolation in later life will create better services for everybody

Much of the current debate around the future of ageing is characterised by a tone of impending doom.[49] Politicians and the media frequently engage in what has been called 'apocalyptic demography', using demographic statistics to 'read off' additional health care or other costs, usually to expose shortcomings in current provision.

Demos has rejected elsewhere this 'time-bomb' appraisal of the ageing society, arguing that future generations of older people will have much to contribute both socially and economically to Britain.[50]

Shifting the way we think about and behave towards those at risk of becoming housebound and socially isolated will be crucial if the contribution of current and future generations of older people is to be maximised.

This will certainly require investment, but of the sort that will ensure more efficient services in the longer term. Take domiciliary care, for example, currently reaching 700,000 older and physically disabled people and an area of service delivery where demand is set to grow.[51] The 1999 Royal Commission on Long Term Care emphasised the need for increased levels of domiciliary care as a way of enabling individuals to maintain their independence for as long as possible. 'Research and experience in this country and elsewhere suggest that, as well as being what people want, providing a larger proportion of care in people's own homes is a practical alternative.'[52]

And yet, while contact hours have risen since 1997, the actual number of households receiving domiciliary care has fallen – reflecting the concentration of these services on those individuals in most extreme need.[53] As the Independent Inquiry into Inequalities in Health found, levels of domiciliary support in the UK are insufficient to stem the tide of older people entering residential care.[54]

This is despite the enormous pay-off of investing in and improving homecare services. At any one time, older people occupy around two-thirds of hospital beds, even though a great many of those patients could be at home if they were better supported. 'Delayed discharge' costs the NHS an estimated £170 million and 1.7 million lost bed days each year.[55] The National Audit Office recently estimated that around 4,100 older patients on any given day are fit enough to leave hospital, but have nowhere appropriate to go.[56]

To be fair, policymakers have been aware of this problem for some time. In 2001 the government drew up the National Service Framework for Older People (NSF) as a 'comprehensive strategy to ensure fair, high quality, integrated health and social care services for older people'. Understanding the potential impact of such joined up delivery on quality of life was at the heart of its message: 'Proper assessment of the range and complexity of older people's needs and prompt provision of care…can improve their ability to function independently, reduce the need for emergency hospital admission and decrease the need for premature admission to a residential care setting.'[57] Furthermore, recent legislation now means that councils that do not provide suitable community care services for patients now incur fines. So why isn't this strategic vision yet a reality?

'Intermediate care' solutions have enormous potential for treating older people in their homes or preventing long hospital stays. 'Hospital at Home' schemes, for example, where they exist, enable early discharge for elderly patients or admission avoidance, thus helping to reduce the pressure on acute hospital beds. The cost of such services in revenue terms is almost certainly neutral, and some studies suggest that admission avoidance schemes might even represent a *less* costly alternative to hospital care.[58] Yet intermediate care remains a relatively under-explored field of practice, often involving complex local partnership arrangements that create challenges for strategic planning, joined up commissioning and effective governance.[59] These are at the crux of current shortcomings in delivery and implementation. Many local authorities, for example, still fail to factor longer-term needs into tender design for specific home care services such as Meals on Wheels, often because of conflicting pressure to demonstrate so-called 'best value'. Senior managers interviewed from WRVS feel that these contracts are often awarded without full consideration of how homecare services can help individuals retain their independence in the longer-term. One of them told us:

> Local authorities have to look at cost, but 'best value' should mean awarding contracts with a longer-term view rather than focusing on paper outputs. A meal delivered to a home is an output, but what's the outcome for the individual? If we work out that, then we have a better chance of keeping that person out of hospital and independent for as long as possible.

The nature of the structures required to support integrated and strategically delivered services is less important than the principles upon which they rest. In other words, what is needed is an explicit policy focus on prevention. This was the view of the Audit Commission in 1997, when it concluded that government had made too little investment in preventative and rehabilitative services, leading to unplanned admissions of older people to hospital and premature admission to long-term residential care.

Again, at national policy level, this lesson has been taken on board. The NSF aims to reduce the incidence of stroke in the population and the number of falls resulting in serious injury (both prevalent among older people), and points to valuable preventative measures such as free flu shots for over-65s and the Keep Warm, Keep Well campaigns, helping to prevent deaths from cold each winter. The Association of Directors of Social Services argues for a model of practice that identifies different types and levels of prevention, from reducing the need for services for relatively healthy people to minimising the requirement for intensive nursing care for those with high support needs.[60] Yet the decision to focus homecare on those in most acute need only has led to unintended consequences that undermine the principle of prevention: 'Given budget constraints, this means that older people with lower levels of need receive less help. The investment has also been at the expense of preventative or promotional "lower level" services.'[61]

Targeting those with lower level needs is exactly what is needed to minimise the risk of isolation for older people. Some of the most important causes of falls, for example, are closely linked to the wider experience of being housebound and unsupported. Poor housing, baths without handles, ill-fitting shoes, unsafe walking areas – these are exactly the sort of disabling conditions that make independent living difficult to achieve, but which could be alleviated with relative ease. Doing so can make the difference between good and poor health. As the NSF recognises, 'chronic degenerative disease, disability and ill health are not an inevitable consequence of ageing'.[62] If older people are given the opportunities to stay fit and active for longer through, for example, tailored exercise programmes such as Tai Chi or chair-based exercise for the very frail, debilitating accidents that reduce quality of life are more likely to be avoided.

At present falls are a major cause of disability in older people aged over 75, and in 2001 over 400,000 older people in England attended A&E departments following exactly these sorts of accidents. Almost half of all women experience an osteoporotic fracture by the time they reach the age of 70. Yet there is ample evidence of the benefits of staying active. The World Health Organisation argues that 'regular physical activity helps to preserve independent living…regular activity helps prevent and/or postpone the age associated declines in balance and coordination that are a major risk factor for falls'. Similarly, the American College of Sports Medicine finds that additional benefits for older people from exercise include 'improved bone health, and, thus, reduction of osteoporosis; improved postural stability, thereby reducing the risk of falling and associated injuries and fractures; and increased flexibility and range of motion'.[63] According to the British Heart Foundation, however, the majority of older people in the UK today remain inactive.

Adding it up: the costs of social isolation among older people

○ Delayed discharges cost the NHS an estimated £170 million and 1.7 million lost bed days each year.

○ In 2001, over 400,000 older people in England attended A&E departments following a slip, trip or fall.

○ Around 4,100 older patients on any given day are fit enough to leave hospital, but have nowhere appropriate to go.

Point 4: By extending years of active life, we enlarge the positive contribution of older people

That prevention should be a priority is nothing new. It must be understood as part of a wider move in shifting the focus of policy and practice away from a 'welfare net' view of the role for government and its social partners and towards a more positive affirmation of quality of life for individuals and their communities. At heart, then, what investing in preventative measures really means is finding ways to extend years of active life among older people. Doing so not only creates pay-offs for core service providers (particularly in the NHS); it enlarges the possibilities for older people to make an active contribution to their families and the wider community. For example, grandparents in the UK spend an average six and a half hours a week caring for their grandchildren, and more than two-thirds of British parents now rely on their own parents to provide some childcare.[64] Older people are keen volunteers too. Research shows that 45 per cent of people aged 65 to 74 and 35 per cent of those over 75 give time regularly across a whole spectrum of activities.[65] Older people get involved in local politics, arts and culture, leisure and other forms of social participation. In other words, they are a rich part of Britain's civil society.

Yet these and other opportunities for living actively and independently must be available to the most at-risk groups of isolated older people. This should be a priority for policymakers. The sustainability of our public services will benefit, not to mention Britain's social (and moral) fabric. Yet to do so will require a whole new way of talking and thinking about the public realm. It is to this task that the next chapter turns.

3. From isolation to personalisation

Summary

Policymakers are increasingly looking to users to secure improvement and innovation in Britain's public services. Yet consultation and
'user engagement' strategies have not yet succeeded in transforming
users into 'co-producers' of key service outcomes such as health or
education. Engaging older housebound people is particularly
challenging because many feel let down by services in the past. The
voluntary and community sectors have a key role to play in bridging
this divide and fostering more innovative forms of inclusion and
participation. This, however, must be positively enabled by the policy
framework for contracting and commissioning social care and other
services used by older people.

The intimate experiences of older housebound people may be hidden
behind their front doors, and yet the larger context in which they are
located – the modernisation of Britain's public services – is a subject
rarely off our television screens, radio waves or newspaper leader
pages. As the previous chapter argued, making the connection
between social isolation and this wider reform agenda is the key to
making the case for sustained change.

In previous eras citizens looked exclusively to governments to take
the lead on making services deliver for users (and to complain to

when those services fail). This mindset still exists among many providers and users. However, of growing significance in the political discourse of recent years is the idea that public service delivery won't improve unless government finds ways to involve users more actively in creating better outcomes.

This idea – that citizens are the most important stakeholders in their own social inclusion and well-being – is now moving to the centre of the debate around public services, and spawning a whole new vocabulary of user empowerment. For example, the Prime Minister's Strategy Unit began exploring the concept of 'co-production' in late 2002 in its paper *Creating Public Value*, discussing how government should move beyond conventional consultation or user engagement into influencing citizen behaviour at a more fundamental level.[66] And in January 2004 Tony Blair laid out a vision of user engagement that conceptualises the citizen as the partner at the very heart of public services reform:

> *We are starting…to understand that service users with high expectations and the power to choose and to be heard are the best drivers of further improvement. By arming the public with greater choice and by strengthening their individual and collective voice we are making them partners in service improvement.*[67]

This vision of public services as a partnership between providers and users offers a broader context in which to understand the growing pressures on public bodies to consult widely and develop new ways of involving service users in the design and delivery of services. This has been a particularly strong theme in programmes and initiatives tackling social exclusion and the government's neighbourhood renewal strategy, which claimed, for the first time to be 'putting residents at the heart of regeneration'. What this reflects is the growing recognition among policymakers that they do not have all the answers to long-standing policy problems, and that achieving step change requires learning from a wide range of stakeholders – including ordinary service users – and developing ways to mobilise them in collective pursuit of shared social outcomes.[68]

As Blair himself pointed out in the same speech:

Parents are key partners in the education of their children. The cooperation of local communities is vital to tackling crime and anti-social behaviour. Employers are key to finding the right jobs for the right people. We can only make real strides in improving the nation's health if citizens themselves lead healthier lifestyles.

This suggests an entirely different role for government and a different relationship with citizens, who no longer are passive recipients of services given the opportunity to express their satisfaction or dissatisfaction only at election time. But instead they become active participants in managing their own lives.

Co-production and the housebound

This message of empowerment supports much of the case for better service delivery for older housebound people made in the previous chapter. For too long, specialist care and mainstream services have constructed users in terms of their problems, seeing them as a set of 'needs', which can be assessed and then met by the right deployment of services. The new paradigm of partnership challenges this model of service delivery by rethinking the respective roles and responsibilities of provider and user. The term used to describe this vision of joint effort and collaboration is 'co-production'. Co-production re-conceptualises the traditional distinction between the provider who produces the service and the user who consumes it. It does this by enlarging the role of the user as a factor in his or her own education, health, employment and so on. The role of the provider is no longer to meet a discrete need – such as prescribing a medicine or delivering a geography lesson – but to develop the capacity of individuals in the longer term to manage their own health or set their own learning goals. The provider and user therefore 'co-produce' the outcome together.

Services supporting those at risk of isolation are ripe for reform along these lines. Users have for too long been left out of the picture: 'Services and projects which aim to support isolated older people are often not providing what older people themselves want.'[69] As long as older people's voices are not heard, their potential to become co-producers will remain untapped. The question remains: what will it take to transform housebound service users into co-producers?

Much has been said in policy debates on health and education of the need to empower citizens as consumers of services by extending choice. This, the government has argued, is the key mechanism for driving up performance, and it is a position with many advocates. But it has its critics, too, many of whom argue that not all citizens are able to choose effectively or exercise their consumer power in a way that best advances their interests. Often it's the most socially excluded or isolated in Britain who face just such a challenge. They are often invisible to service providers and other authorities, and government struggles to reach them via mainstream delivery mechanisms. Equally, attempts to involve them through consultation or community engagement exercises or new forms of local governance such as partnership boards often fail, because those methods are not sufficiently sensitive to the multiple barriers to participation that they face.

Older people want to be involved in planning, developing and delivering activities that target social isolation and loneliness.[70] And, to be fair, older service users are in a stronger position to do so than ever before, with the extension of direct payments and the focus on giving users a greater voice in the National Service Framework 'Better Government for Older People'; this partnership, created to promote learning among service providers, exists primarily 'to ensure older people are engaged as citizens at all levels of decision-making', and holds as its key partner an Older People's Advisory Group, composed of ordinary older service users.

Yet engaging and involving the most marginalised users requires particular creativity and a long-term view. Older housebound people, as we have seen, often resist external interventions for complex emotional and psychological reasons. Taking time to build trust between provider and user is crucial if these barriers are to be broken down and housebound people are to take on the role of co-producers.

In the past, little attempt has been made to investigate the meaning of isolation and loneliness to older people themselves (something that the ESRC Growing Older Programme is trying to address), especially with regard to the 'identity work' that shapes how older people respond to offers of assistance. Agreeing to receive a service is often incompatible with an individual's personal projects to fight, delay and even deny need. In this light, the technocratic tools of 'needs assessment' appear to negate the personal biographies of older people by reducing them to the sum of their abilities and disabilities. So just what can policymakers do to ensure that all service users, including older housebound people, have the opportunity to become co-producers?

Using the voluntary sector as a gateway to the isolated

To a great extent, the answer lies beyond Whitehall or the local authority and in the realm of civil society. Shortly after coming into government Tony Blair talked about the need 'to steer rather than row', reflecting his belief that government should no longer represent the key deliverer, but instead the expert broker, highly skilled at managing relationships and drawing on the knowledge and capacities of other actors in the system.

Certainly this vision has ensured the continued expansion of private sector provision, but it has also enlarged possibilities for the voluntary and community sector (VCS) to play a greater role in service delivery. The key rationale behind this expanded role is that the VCS has distinctive qualities, which allow it to outperform other providers in many service areas, namely, its local knowledge, the level of trust it is able to build with users, its perceived independence from political control, and its capacity for social innovation. The evidence points strongly to the superiority of the sector in reaching vulnerable individuals in certain social policy fields, especially where VCS organisations have achieved a strong 'rootedness' in local social ecologies.[71]

Transforming users into the co-producers of improved service delivery is an enormous cultural challenge for government, which has, since the creation of the modern welfare state, preferred to shape users to services. Many voluntary sector organisations therefore are better placed in this regard, particularly those with a strong empowerment agenda and experience in community capacity building. Yet turning to the VCS provides no tidy solution for the housebound. As the role of the sector has increased, so too have the pressures and constraints upon it with regard to targets, performance management and financial accountability – in other words, the conventional auditing grounds of efficiency and cost-effectiveness favoured by government.

While all voluntary providers support the need for high standards and quality control, many feel that the emphasis on accountability upwards to local authorities, central government and ultimately ministers can compromise their ability to respond to the needs of users and to pioneer innovative practice in order to do so. A good example of this is the Meals on Wheels service delivered to the homes of thousands of housebound people across Britain. WRVS has been a key provider of Meals on Wheels for decades, with its body of 95,000 volunteers currently delivering around nine million meals each year. The daily social contact between the volunteer who delivers the meal and the housebound user is central to the service, facilitating friendly exchange and providing opportunities for the user to voice concerns or ask for help with simple tasks, as well as access information about other services and activities. However, a growing number of local authorities are now choosing to contract frozen meal delivery services, which typically involve a delivery to the home once a fortnight.

While this may appear to achieve cost-savings and greater efficiency, it also carries the risk of reinforcing social isolation through the loss of daily contact between users and providers. Furthermore, by privileging what might appear to be convenience and choice in meal delivery above all else, this sort of strategy risks missing what older housebound people really want and need from services more broadly. By providing the Meals on Wheels service, WRVS aims to empower housebound people and support independent living. However, many housebound people are able to prepare and cook their own meals. Their main problem is in getting to the shops and carrying heavy bags of groceries home. For these individuals, the Meals on Wheels service in its current role arguably *inhibits* co-production by placing them in an unnecessarily passive role. What would be more effective would be an assisted shopping or assisted cooking service. Yet because domiciliary care services are not currently measured against the goals of co-production, it is not easy for VCS organisations such as WRVS to innovate in this direction, however much this might be in the interests of their users.

Personalisation: changing the script

What has become increasingly clear over the last decade is the extent to which VCS organisations aspire to be treated as professionals with high levels of expertise and knowledge who are fully engaged in the creation and development of evidence-based policy. As the next chapter will show, this expertise and knowledge with regard to meeting the needs of the housebound is considerable. Yet the task of applying it to the wider co-production agenda will require working with government to create an infrastructure of integrated and adaptive services with the capacity to shape themselves around the needs of unique users.

The concept of 'citizen-centred' services is not a new one, dating back to the early 1990s with 'one-stop shops' and the Citizen's Charter. 'Joined-up government' became the mantra of New Labour after 1997, and led to the breaking down of arbitrary organisational boundaries and the creation of new forms of cross-cutting action and multi-agency working to support the aspiration of seamless service delivery.

These principles for modernisation have helped to shift the balance of power away from producers and towards users, but have stopped short of turning those users into co-producers, still seeing them as essentially consumers of (albeit reconfigured) services. Yet if co-production becomes a widely understood concept, informing service design and delivery across all areas of provision, it has the potential to achieve at a more fundamental level what many are now calling the 'personalisation' of Britain's public services.[72] Demos author Charlie Leadbeater describes this as 'bottom-up, mass social innovation, enabled by the state', and argues that personalisation could become as compelling an idea in reshaping public provision over the next decade as privatisation was in the 1980s and 1990s.[73]

Innovation of this kind requires producers and users to adopt a different 'script' in their interactions. Most services, as Leadbeater argues, can be understood as scripts, where various actors have set roles to play within a familiar narrative, whether that's the sequence of events that characterises a student's school day or a patient's visit to the GP. As we have seen, most older housebound people know their lines off by heart: their role usually involves waiting for the tap at the door of the home help or the Meals on Wheels van, or following the instructions on their medical prescriptions.

The task of transforming housebound service users into co-producers writing their own scripts is about engaging housebound people in more sophisticated ways. It should be based on action in the following three areas: in the home, in the community and reaching people most in need.

In the home

The script for service delivery to older housebound people should be an open-ended dialogue, which takes the user as its starting point. Services that focus on predefined 'problems' can miss important aspirations or emotional issues, which need to inform the design of those services. For example, a person who has been isolated for many years may take a long time to build up the courage to agree to participate in a group activity. If they are then put on a waiting list – as is often the case – and given no interim support, this let-down can seriously set them back. These and other services need to find ways of giving users real voice in expressing what is important to them, and real power in shaping the nature of the services they receive.

In the community

The script for older housebound people is not confined to the individual user and a single provider. Parts are played by many other actors both in the individual's family and his or her wider community. Providers that do not recognise this wider nexus of relationships effectively turn the script into a two-hander, with opportunities missed for using services as a way of drawing individuals into a wider orbit of social participation. For example, many older people receive formal care, but are also – or would like to be – carers themselves, either for disabled partners or grandchildren, or through voluntary work of various kinds.

Reaching people most in need

Reducing the number of people who partially, or totally, exclude themselves from valuable sources of support is an essential task of making co-production a reality for all older housebound people. Part of the answer is about improving services to make them more attractive. However, more attention needs to be paid to the actual experience of becoming a service user – in terms of needs assessment, form filling, communication and relationship building – and how this overall process affects self-esteem, engagement and the ability to co-produce. Understanding how channels into support can become more innovative, more attuned to diverse needs and broader in their scope for engaging housebound people should become a priority task for service providers and housebound people themselves.

4. Principles for personalisation

Summary

While there are constraints and barriers to developing personalised services, there are plenty of examples of good practice where users are genuinely empowered to become co-producers of their care and wider inclusion. These range from inclusive design and use of interactive technology to peer networking and volunteering opportunities for older people. Drawn largely from the voluntary and community sector, these provide useful learning points for transformation of the wider system.

This chapter will develop a vision of what co-production might look like in the field of service for housebound people, drawing on examples of best practice and innovation. These examples are drawn from a wide range of providers, and do not assume that responsibility lies with a single source.

In the home

By listening to housebound people's views, solutions to some of the difficulties of providing services within and outside the home can begin to be uncovered. However, listening is not an easy or straight-forward process. Listening encompasses many different processes and techniques as diverse as focused research programmes, political processes and advocacy, interactive data flows, and whole cultural approach of service providers. This section outlines some of the ways in which services within the home have been, or could be, designed around older housebound people's views and aspirations.

Design of homes and the physical environment

Design for the young and you exclude the old; design for the old and you include the young
> *(the late Bernard Isaacs, Founding Director of the Birmingham Centre for Applied Gerontology).*

The design of the physical environment is an example of a service that is necessarily outsourced to 'experts', but can be made more effective by understanding design in terms of the overall experience, as well as practical functionality. The positive associations of the home are crucial to the self-esteem of an older housebound person, and policy must support these connections wherever possible. Julienne Hanson, a homes expert based at UCL, used a variety of research tools, including focus groups, in-depth interviews, detailed ethnographies of older people's home life and questionnaires to understand older people's relationships with their homes. She found that most older people want to live in a normal family house, and few opt for the purpose-built 'special needs' alternative, which is often cramped and combines intimate and service spaces (for instance, combining the bedroom and living room).

There is a danger that although normal family homes may help older housebound people feel more integrated in mainstream society, such homes are typically very disabling for frail people, with difficult entrances, inappropriate fixtures and fittings and first-floor bathrooms. Julienne Hanson argues that some homes 'evict' their occupants, when they could still continue independent living in a better designed space.[74]

This research has contributed to the vision of inclusive design. Inclusive design, also know as 'universal design' and 'design for all', proposes that any space should be visitable or usable by anyone, no matter whether they are disabled, elderly, or young children. An essential premise of inclusive design is the inclusion of users in the design process. A good example of how this can work to the advantage of older housebound people is provided by Encompass, a partnership between Dark Horse Venture and WRVS. This scheme facilitates Access Assessment groups, where housebound people visit country houses to review provision for disabled access.

Inclusive design can also incorporate 'smart' technologies, which aim to facilitate independent living. For example, the book *Digital Futures*, produced by the Chartered Institute of Housing, outlines a vision of an interactive house for older people. In this vision hi-tech 'smart' homes monitor movement in the environment, activate alarms, predict and prevent accidents, analyse lifestyle patterns and give feedback so that the system is continuously improved. Technical health care solutions diagnose and monitor symptoms from home, as well as transmit data and images to and from home and the surgery or hospital. Advocates of telemedicine and e-health rarely propose that hi-tech health solutions can or should replace human interaction. However, it is clear that they can ease housebound people's worries about accidents and emergencies, as well as making the information that passes housebound people and their service providers more accessible and transparent.[75] Clearly the potential to achieve this vision is as yet unrealised.

Interactive technology

For some housebound people new technology is already improving their quality of life. Both public institutions and commercial providers have begun to make their offerings more inclusive. Many older and ethnic minority groups enjoy television and DVDs with the benefit of subtitles in a multitude of different languages. The 2002 Communications Bill regulated that in ten years' time it will be compulsory for 90 per cent of output from ITV, Channel 4 and Five, and 80 per cent of the output of all other digital channels, to be subtitled for the benefit of deaf and hard of hearing people.

Technology is set to become more important for all of society as government aims to ensure that all government services are accessible electronically by the end of 2005. However, as we have already seen, not all older people have the access to technology, or indeed the confidence to learn the new skills required to use ICTs and benefit fully from the e-services on offer.

One initiative that has helped overcome these barriers is the Laptop Initiative, a partnership between DfES, NIACE and the Basic Skills Agency, which provides laptops to community groups. What makes this initiative different from others is that it does not define a desired outcome in advance and allows individuals to develop at their own pace with the support of additional resources. The progress that is made is then reported at a later stage. One of the projects funded by the initiative provided one-to-one adult education for disabled people in their own homes. In this case, housebound learners are partnered with volunteer tutors who attend weekly college classes, and then relay their learning to the housebound partners later on. In this way both partners are learning together in a relaxed yet sustained way.

Technology continues to hold out much promise for increasing the quality of life for those with limited mobility outside their homes. Investing in skills development and innovative locally-based projects is likely to have a 'multiplier' effect for those users, as they will be able to access crucial information, services and advice, such as home shopping, support groups and further learning opportunities.

Home services

Services delivered to people in the home can be a real lifeline. However, sometimes services can act to reinforce isolation by making it unnecessary to leave the home, and by preventing older house-bound people from achieving things for themselves.

Currently the difference between understanding where home services are working and where they are not is difficult to identify. Policy is not sufficiently informed by what independence really means to older housebound people. Independence is not a simplistic notion of physical mobility and self-sufficiency, but a more involved idea incorporating choice, dignity, decision-making and enjoyment, and this definition may vary considerably by individual. As one wheelchair user expressed it: 'Some people may think, you know, that

I'm not independent because I can't do it for myself. I can't go to town by myself. I don't see independent living that way. I see independent living as I make the decision.'76

A wide range of services developed by organisations such as WRVS and Help the Aged demonstrate how services can support people in their homes. For example, Help the Aged HandyVan service provides trained fitters who visit the home and install security fittings, such as door chains and viewers, window locks and smoke detectors. Help the Aged also runs gardening assistance schemes for older people. Another service is SeniorLink, the immediate response service. Through the touch of a button, help is on hand to assist with emergencies, or simply for people to hear a reassuring voice. The presence of these services is crucial in the overall support structure for older housebound people. As the population ages, these services are likely to become more important. One way in which they can be enhanced and become more universal could be through changes in how purchasing authorities assess 'value', for example by upgrading the importance of reducing isolation. This idea is discussed further in the recommendations.

The key to continuous improvement in home services does not lie only with local authorities. Services themselves need to develop and innovate by creating more systematic feedback loops between services and users, and through greater opportunities for users to influence the form of the services.

A good example of how home services can become personalised is WRVS's Good Neighbours schemes, which put vulnerable older people, especially those who have recently returned from hospital, in touch with volunteers able to complete small tasks such as shopping, collecting pensions, or being present when workmen visit. These kinds of services are likely to be more flexible, responsive and less passive for the housebound person than many other kinds of centrally-controlled services. The overall process helps to develop and increase local capacity for older housebound people – in other words, creating ways in which they can be the co-producers of their own quality of life.

In the community

Social contact with others can be very empowering for older housebound people. Research shows that participating in voluntary groups and social activities can extend years of healthy life and reduce depression.[77] But not just any social activity will do. One study found that the older people who were surveyed stressed the importance 'of shared age, culture, interests, personal history and background' in providing quality contact with supportive groups.[78] Many older people resent the assumption made by some providers of day care or other services in the community that people aged over 65 will enjoy the same pursuits and each other's company. The best services offer opportunities for older people to design their own programme of activities and forge their own friendships and social connections.

Two such spaces are provided by Age Concern's 'Baby Boomer Bistro', and Contact the Elderly. What these two very different projects share in common is their refusal to prescribe specific solutions to frailty or isolation. Their remit instead is simply to create opportunities for people to get together with others like them. Baby Boomer Bistro is an internet chat room dedicated for older people. Quiz sessions are held on Wednesday and Friday afternoons, and other times are used for general chat and discussions. In 2004 members of the site went on holiday together to Hayling Island, posting up the photographs for other users to see.[79]

A very different service is provided by Contact the Elderly, a charitable organisation facilitating gatherings for frail, elderly people who live alone. One Sunday afternoon a month, volunteer drivers take elderly people on regular visits to hosts' homes. Friends can then sit and chat over tea. For many users the experience can be more homely than alternatives in a special centre, and relationships can flourish between elderly people and their assigned drivers.

Transport services

The ease with which older housebound people participate in wider social groups frequently lies in the community transport sector. The gaps in mainstream provision of public transport mean that housebound people often end up relying on this sector to get to day care centres, lunch clubs and other social groups. The community transport sector is large but relatively hidden. According to the Community Transport Association, there are over 100,000 minibuses serving over ten million passengers every year being operated for use by voluntary, community and public groups, or to provide door-to-door transport for housebound people.[80] New government tax concessions on fuel are helping community transport suppliers reach more people. Ealing Community Transport, for example, has a fleet of 30 minibuses providing low cost, high quality transport for community groups. It estimates that the fuel rebate of 40p per litre will enable the organisation to invest an extra £1,000 per month into providing better services.

However, there is still a need for services to be more flexible and localised. Housebound people's transport needs are frequently fairly modest, but the simple changes in provision that could make the world of difference are not being provided. Researchers from Leeds reported one older wheelchair user who was offered transport to a community centre but not to reach a close friend who lived in the same street. During Demos research for this study, we visited a housebound woman who asked us to fetch a paper from the local shop – literally yards from her house.[81] Allowing housebound people to express their own transport needs is essential. For example, Help the Aged's Senior Mobility Programme helps local groups and projects tailor-make their own transport solutions by providing funds for a variety of transport equipment, from manual and electric wheelchairs to scooters, electric buggies and community cars. These kinds of solutions are likely to be more flexible in terms of creating the transport solutions that housebound people need.

Volunteering or employment opportunities

The benefits of volunteering for older people has received a great deal of interest from policymakers over the last few years. In 2000 the then Performance and Innovation Unit produced a report called *Winning the Generation Game*, which called for government to help 'older people to make use of their skills and experience for the benefit of the wider community'.[82] This resulted in 2002 in the creation of the 'Experience Corps', set up as an independent, non-profit making company, funded by a grant-in-aid from the Home Office, which seeks to match the skills and experience of the over-50s to needs in Britain's communities. Another similarly targeted programme is the Retired and Senior Volunteer Programme (RSVP), which is part of Community Service Volunteers and aims to encourage 60-year-olds and upwards to become active in their communities.

RSVP enables older people to express their often untapped interest in their communities and play a larger role in ongoing regeneration and community development initiatives. One recent study warns that 'the policy-making process is missing out on the potentially enormous contribution that older people appear willing to make to influence the development of their neighbourhoods'.[83] One way of ensuring that older housebound people have the opportunity to make just such a contribution as co-producers of better neighbourhoods is by designing volunteering programmes that appeal to and are appropriate for those with limited mobility.

What gives RSVP its strengths compared to many other volunteering programmes is in the way that it enables volunteers to group together and decide which parts of their community to support, and when and how to do it. Current projects include knitting clothes for premature babies and mentoring children in schools. If RSVP and other voluntary organisations continue to push at common understandings of what constitutes 'volunteering', then older housebound people have every chance of being able to play an active role. It is likely, however, that policymakers will have to work harder to engage future generations of older people in volunteering. A survey by the Office for National Statistics showed that 39 per cent of the current over-55 age group supported the statement 'everyone has a duty to do voluntary work at some time in their lives', whereas only 26.5 per cent of the younger babyboomers agreed.[84] This has implications not only for future older people needing sustained social support networks in local areas, but also on major service providers such as WRVS and Age Concern who rely on volunteers as part of their structure. One potentially effective way of reaching new volunteers, as well as those in need, is through peer network schemes, to which the next section turns.

Reaching people most in need

Our analysis suggests that there is a whole contingent of individuals who are not accessing services. Physical barriers to support are important, but so are emotional ones. These people can miss out in a variety of ways, for example by not picking up their pensions, not visiting their doctor, and not referring themselves or being referred to the valuable home services offered by voluntary, public or private providers. Sometimes these omissions are caused by serious difficulties in accessing transport, or understanding information. Very often, however, older housebound people reject outside help in order to maintain their independent identities and self-esteem – though this may prove more damaging in the long term.

Managing the process into support needs to be done very sensitively in terms of how support is offered, who by and how.

Routes into support

There is not one route into providing support for housebound people. The experience of asking for, receiving and giving help needs to be designed so that the diversity of need can be expressed, the barriers to participation are low, and ways of working are flexible.

One example where these principles have been taken on can be found at Age Concern Stockport. This group set up its Wellcheck project based on evidence that showed how many housebound people were missing out on services because those services were not alerted to their needs, or because they fell outside strict social care eligibility criteria. The project takes the individual as a starting point, making no presumptions of need, but instead asks users what might help and then designs services around their answers. Clients can choose between home visits and telephone contact, and then can ask for how much help they need in setting services up. One popular service is Easyshop, where clients without internet access receive a weekly phone call to order shopping, and then their chosen supermarket delivers to their door. Feedback indicates that the friendly phone call is as important as the service itself.

Services like Wellcheck reach vulnerable people, but are reliant on effective referrals. Yet older people often resist referring themselves because of fears about dependence and perceived neediness. Sometimes the needs of older people are simply not picked up. In these cases, the best route into support is often through a familiar and trusted source. Research shows that older housebound people tend to want to maintain continuity in terms of long-term relationships and social contacts rather than being asked to replace them. Where new sources of support become essential, introducing them through existing and familiar contacts is best.

This is where support services in the home such as Meals on Wheels, home library services and Good Neighbours schemes provide an essential channel of information and advice. By seeing people regularly and helping with minor household tasks, those visiting housebound people can also keep up to date with what extra services they might need or be entitled to. Older people are inclined to find a familiar face more approachable and trustworthy than someone they haven't met before, especially when that person is a volunteer.

Peer networks

Volunteers can introduce services to housebound people in a friendly and approachable way. Another more radical approach to service provision is by turning service users into volunteers themselves through peer network schemes. Telephone services manned by housebound people are one way in which this has been achieved. The Listening Eye, for example, is a national telephone helpline for those having difficulty with their eyesight. It is staffed by people with a visual impairment themselves and a wide experience of coming to terms with it. The Listening Eye can be an important first port of call for people noticing problems with their vision, but who are unwilling to trigger a full-scale medical process or want to talk about aspects of their experience to someone who is not a doctor.

Another example of a peer network is the Someone Like Me! Senior Peer Health Mentoring and local physical activity programmes, which is a national programme and a partnership between Ageing Well UK and the British Heart Foundation National Centre for Physical Activity and Health. Based on the US model CHAMPS, the programme is inspired by the evidence that exercise among older people can improve balance, reduce falls and cost less than medical interventions. However, barriers to exercise can be substantial for older people and include beliefs and fears about overdoing it, or 'it's too late for me'. The problem of inactivity among the older population is widespread. One study estimates that 86 per cent of older women and 78 per cent of older men in care homes are inactive.[85] The Senior Peer Mentor Physical Activity Motivator Programme uses mentors to encourage older adults of all ages to take up regular physical activity. Mentors provide information and can talk about their own exercise experiences. They do not give medical advice, or lead physical activity, yet simply providing people with a positive role model can prove more effective than other kinds of health promotion work.

These examples show how services for older housebound people can be developed to be more in tune with what they want and need to help them continue being at the heart of their own quality of life. The next Chapter turns to how policy can help meet the challenge of loneliness for the next generation of older housebound people.

5. Conclusions and recommendations

So far our analysis has shown that the risk of becoming lonely, especially in later life, is increasing. Many of the factors contributing to this increase are actually associated with positives in our lives such as greater personal choice, geographical mobility and longevity.

Loneliness should not be the penance paid by some for the success of society overall. The associated costs of loneliness affect everybody. Medical costs for treating the common symptoms of loneliness such as falls and fractures, depression and poor immunity are vast. Of course, some of this is caused by inevitable frailty in older age. But too often these health complaints are the direct result of isolated people living unsupported and demotivating lives. The social cost of loneliness is also large. Isolated people who do not contribute to community life represent a huge resource of untapped potential. Friends and relatives are affected too, and worry about how to ask for help, or how to cope.

The problem is not that loneliness is inevitable, but that our social response has been inadequate. From the older isolated person's perspective, often the opportunities to relieve loneliness and isolation are so insufficient that the best strategy seems to be to deny the problem altogether.

Some improvements have been made. Local authorities are now judged on how effective they are at enabling older people to stay living independently in their homes. There has also been a new focus on getting social care and health authorities to work together, though controversy still exists on how this might be achieved. However, too often services fail to engage and motivate older housebound citizens, and remain focused on the functional provision for physical needs. A broader social response is needed to allow older housebound people to play a part in their own quality of life. The government investment in civic renewal and active communities is right but, so far, older housebound people have remained hidden from these agendas.

Ultimately, 'housebound' as a category of disadvantage and a variation on the theme of isolation will fade away and be replaced by independent living as a positive identity and an active choice on the part of older people. This is because in the future the world outside the front door will be structured in ways – physically and socially – that create opportunities for all, regardless of age or level of mobility. This is a fundamental part of the vision of personalised public services, generated and sustained through forms of provision, which enable professionals, volunteers and service users to co-produce better social outcomes together.

We recommend the following actions on the part of government, the voluntary sector and business to help make this vision a reality.

Change the criteria for commissioning social care

The criteria for commissioning social care for older housebound people need to be changed to include co-production indicators. Social care decisions and judgements about performance are currently based on relatively narrow datasets related to needs assessment and cost efficiency. We have shown how care is most effective (and cost-efficient) where it is based upon the goal of reducing loneliness. We have also shown that the best way to reduce loneliness is to engage people in co-producing their own quality of life. How then can these findings be incorporated into the criteria by which social care decisions are made?

We argue that the VCS should take the lead in developing information-gathering techniques and service performance indicators. The principal way in which this process can be achieved is by giving service users more opportunities for communication and feedback. Already the WRVS Meals on Wheels service operates as an information service by delivering leaflets on subjects such as fuel benefits. This idea should be extended by enabling a wider range of home care services to provide extra information and opportunities for feedback.

VCS providers do not historically have a strength in managing information and knowledge. However, they are perceived to have a better understanding of the diverse kinds of value created during social care interactions, such as friendship, identity maintenance, motivation and information sharing. This is why VCS providers are best placed to pioneer new ways of measuring social care commissioning, which could then be transferred to other kinds of providers.

Voluntary service providers might have concerns that increasing the opportunities for feedback might raise expectations, which will then be difficult to fulfil. However, what makes daily life interesting is contained in the conversation of small details, such as the quality of a meal, the style of a haircut, the temperature of the house or the ending of a book. Managed well, an ongoing conversation with older people about what makes life better will be invaluable to service providers, as well as helping older people to feel at home with their own lives, and with those that support them.

Community centres serving older housebound people

There should be community centres serving older housebound people in each of the top ten per cent most disadvantaged wards. At worst, spending the day at a day care centre for older people is perceived as stultifying and degrading. At best, contact with such centres can be an empowering route out of isolation for vulnerable older people. What makes the difference between these two experiences?

We argue that really good day care centres for older housebound people aim to increase support for people across a wide variety of locations, and transfer quality of life improvements between a central location and the home.

One excellent example of a centre doing just that can be found in Hanley at the WRVS community centre. This centre is the hub for a large-scale Meals on Wheels service as well as providing food and staff support for nine social clubs. The centre's supported care service offers tailored activity programmes that frequently enable older people to volunteer their time and skills through activities such as fundraising and arts and crafts. In many cases this encourages people to continue with their hobbies at home. Services originating from, or supported by, the centre can be found all over the local area, including in village halls, further education colleges and at the centre's specially-designed allotment garden. Non-housebound people are also attracted to the centre by the busy café operating there.

Unfortunately, examples of really good day care centres are rare, and the overall picture is one of staff struggling against the odds to deliver opportunities to older housebound people. This is even more the case in disadvantaged communities where private services are less accessible and affordable.

Government should reinvigorate centres that are able to increase support for older people throughout the community by funding excellence centres in care for older housebound people in ten per cent of the most disadvantaged wards by 2010. These would be based on the Hanley model and combine inclusive design with imaginative services for older housebound people that are more in line with their hobbies, interests and aspirations. The goal of the new excellence centres would be to empower older housebound people in co-producing their own quality of life, and to engage them in preventative health activities. Transparent forms of monitoring and assessment could spread best practice throughout the sector, and help outline how partnerships between local authority and voluntary sector can work best.

Mainstream age into regeneration policy and delivery

A real indicator of regeneration should be enabling people to get out of their homes and enjoy their communities. There has been much progress in this area, in terms of including older people more actively, not only as users of services but in the strategic planning and governance of regeneration initiatives.[86] However, while older people are well represented where activities have a health or inter-generational focus, they have much less of a voice in areas such as city and town centre renewal. This needs to change. The design of the urban environment has an enormous impact on opportunities for mobility and patterns of sociability, and older people at risk of isolation deserve to have their voices heard.

As we have seen, consultation activities accompanying regeneration strategies are a move in the right direction, but empowering older housebound people as active participants in planning the future of their neighbourhoods is a long way off. At worst some older housebound people believe they no longer have a part to play in the community, ensuring that their social visibility drops even further. Overcoming the physical and psychological barriers to taking part in community life is a massive task. However, as we have seen through the examples in Chapter 4, there is no reason why even the frailest individuals cannot participate in all kinds of community activities, as long as the right kind of support is there for them to access them.

We recommend therefore that government departments developing policy on regeneration and the principal delivery agencies should ensure that age monitoring is mainstreamed throughout all their activities. This should be included in systems of performance management around planning, design and delivery of services. Furthermore, all regeneration bids and decisions about the renewal of town centres should be 'age-proofed' to ensure inclusive futures for all.

The VCS should aid this task by promoting capacity-building activities among older people who could benefit from getting involved in local governance structures in this area such as those found in the New Deal for Communities programme, Health Action Zones and projects funded by the Single Regeneration Budget among others.

Government review of community transport provision

The Social Exclusion Unit recently completed a study of transport and social exclusion, which contained many welcome recommendations about how to make public transport services more inclusive.

Discussion of more specific services focused largely on getting people to work, to school, to hospital or to food shops, neglecting the social and emotional needs of seeing friends and family or meeting new people, which become crucial in later life.[87]

This gap is filled by any number of community transport schemes provided by local voluntary organisations, offering flexible and friendly door-to-door services to older people. They represent a gateway into the wider community, yet provision is fragmented and most schemes struggle to secure long-term funding. Therefore, we recommend that the Social Exclusion Unit commissions a follow-up study of the community transport sector, with a focus on older people and social isolation. This should map current provision and point towards options for strategic development supported by sustainable funding streams. The Community Transport Association should be a key partner in this work, along with major providers and users.

Home from hospital mentors

Older housebound people's quality of life is enhanced if their communities have the ability to find localised ways to swap favours, caring needs, tasks and wisdom. Volunteering schemes can be an ideal way to generate these kinds of personalised networks and can help to transfer these benefits between home, family and community. However, volunteering with older housebound people is not always straightforward and the focus of what is being offered is sometimes unclear. Befriending schemes can be a lifeline for some, but for others the implication of vulnerability can be damaging to self-esteem.

We recommend that a new commitment to mentoring from voluntary sector and government should be focused on older people who come home after a spell in hospital. This would be an ideal way to help maximise the relevance of volunteering to older people. Mentoring is traditionally associated with younger people or with high-flying business executives. We argue that mentoring should be for older people too. Negotiating the house with a new hip, or getting used to cataract-free eyes can be a real learning experience. The Home

Office has already supplied £800,000 for developing a national mentoring and befriending infrastructure body. We recommend that additional funds are made available to enable a closer focus on hospital-home transitions.

Mentors would not be there to act as health care advisors, but they would be able to provide invaluable support, especially if they were familiar with the hospital experience themselves. A mentoring scheme could also help prevent lapses into new periods of ill health in the longer term.

Of course help is already available for older people returning home from hospital. Social services and health care work together to create home care packages. However, often these services are paid for, and are only available for a very limited period. Many hospitals already have voluntary mentoring and befriending schemes, but very often their offer is limited and fragmented. A more focused national scheme could enable mentors to be offered for a full six months after the hospital discharge.

Social exclusion unit taskforce

Britain's housebound population is known only through limited social services data. Yet, as this report has argued, it is a category of disadvantage that reaches much further than those figures would imply, and has a set of meanings that go deeper than reliance on Meals on Wheels or eligibility for a day care place. We recommend therefore that the Social Exclusion Unit launch an investigation of the prevalence of housebound status among older people, disabled people and other risk groups described in this report.

Housebound people benefit particularly from well-designed and appropriately delivered domiciliary services. But we have seen that not all provision places the user at the centre of service delivery. We recommend that the government establishes a cross-cutting, cross-sector taskforce, led by older housebound people themselves, to look at opportunities for improving domiciliary care and other services to the home. This taskforce will develop a set of guidelines to help all providers carry out 'housebound-proofing' – that is, ensuring that their services are designed in ways that move users further towards independence rather than maintaining their housebound status.

Boost for housebound-friendly businesses

As we have discussed, the VCS is best placed to lead best practice in creating personalised services for older housebound people. We should not forget, however, that businesses also plays a crucial role in providing positive outcomes for older housebound people, through inclusively designed products, services delivered to the home, and welcoming venues in the community. These services deliver low cost, stigma free improvements to quality of life as well as regular social contact. Many of these businesses are successful, but there are also many that are at risk of failing or working below their potential, especially in rural or disadvantaged communities.

Business Link, the practical advisory service for business supported by the Department for Trade and Industry, should lead a large-scale survey into how businesses are delivering to older housebound people. This information should then feed into a free training and advice service specifically for businesses that could maximise their business potential through more effective service design and marketing to housebound and older people.

Business innovation can make a positive difference to older house-bound people's lives, but there are also examples of where life is made difficult through inconsiderate consumer services or products. The introduction of tiny 5p pieces is an example of a product designed without the older person in mind, whereas the new 'big' BT phone is clearly an exemplar of good design. The National Consumer Council, or another consumer body, should raise the profile of products that confound, confuse or irritate through the naming and shaming of business culprits, and through the congratulation of best practice.

Promotion of volunteering to over-65s

We recommend that voluntary organisations commit to playing a greater role in promoting active citizenship among the older housebound population. The core goal of many organisations such as

Age Concern, Help the Aged, WRVS, and numerous religious and community groups is to improve the lives and independence of older housebound people, so there is a risk this sounds too obvious. However, enabling the recipients of voluntary services to play an active role in the organisations that facilitate help is not straightforward. Often older housebound people can lapse into being passive recipients of care, no matter how admirable the mission statement or how good the intentions of the volunteers.

One practical way in which the voluntary sector can best enable active participation or 'co-production' is for volunteering organisations actively to promote volunteering among the over-65s. There is already £600,000 from government to go to the development of a national co-ordinating body for older volunteers (filling the gap left by the Experience Corps). However, promoting volunteering to older age groups cannot be the task of a single body, and in fact well-established and trusted brands such as the Women's Institute, Salvation Army and Leonard Cheshire may well have more leverage in encouraging older people to volunteer. Already many of these organisations have a track record in attracting older volunteers and for some the recruitment drive has turned to attracting a younger and more diverse volunteer base. This is important and momentum on new volunteers and greater diversity should be maintained. However, we also recommend that all volunteering organisations, and especially those with expertise in attracting older volunteers, should commit to promoting volunteering among the over-65s and, where possible, find new volunteering opportunities, for instance operating telephones, which are suitable for older housebound people to undertake. Maintaining contact and communications with volunteers who have become housebound and are unable to continue volunteering should also become a more explicit policy.

Notes

1   The National Service Framework is a ten-year programme of action launched by the government in 2001 to ensure high quality and integrated health and social care services for older people.
2   *With Respect to Old Age: long term care – rights and responsibilities* was published in March 1999 as the final report of the Royal Commission on Long Term Care. The Commission's terms of reference were to examine the long- and short-term options for a sustainable system of long-term care for elderly people, both in their homes and in other settings.
3   The Government Actuary Department states that the projected population of those aged 65 and over in 2021 is 12,736,000. If social isolation continues at its current rate (17 per cent of over-65s as calculated by the ESRC Growing Older Programme, Research Findings 17) we can conclude that 2,165,120 people of this age group will be socially isolated, as defined by not being in weekly contact with friends, family or neighbours.
4   NAO, *Ensuring the Effective Discharge of Older Patients from NHS Acute Hospitals* (London: National Audit Office, 2003).
5   C Victor, A Bowling, J Bond and S Scambler, *Loneliness, Social Isolation and Living Alone in Later Life*, ESRC Growing Older Programme, Research Findings 17 (Sheffield: GOP, University of Sheffield, 2003). Available at www.shef.ac.uk/uni/projects/gop/ChristinaVic_F17.pdf.
6   M Castells, *The Rise of the Network Society*, 2nd ed (Oxford: Blackwell, 2000).
7   R Putnam, *Bowling Alone: the collapse and revival of American community* (New York: Simon & Schuster, 2000).
8   P Hall, 'Social capital: a fragile asset', *Demos Collection* 12 (1997).
9   Victor et al, *Loneliness, Social Isolation and Living Alone in Later Life*, ESRC Growing Older Programme, Research Findings 17.
10   See the classic studies by Tunstall in 1963/4; it involved counting weekly total social contacts and identifying a cut-off point to determine isolation.
11   Information published from the *Census 2001 National Report* on 7 May 2003, available at www.statistics.gov.uk/cci/nugget.asp?id=350.

12 S Arber and J Ginn, 'Ageing and gender: diversity and change', *Social Trends*, no 34 (2004).

13 Victor et al, *Loneliness, Social Isolation and Living Alone in Later Life*, ESRC Growing Older Programme, Research Findings 17.

14 C Attwood, G Singh, D Prime, R Creasey et al *2001 Home Office Citizenship Survey: people, families and communities*, Home Office Research Study 270 (London, Home Office, 2003).

15 A Park, J Curtice, K Thomson, L Jarvis and C Bromley, *British Social Attitudes: the 19th report* (London: National Centre for Social Research and SAGE Publications, 2002).

16 Ibid.

17 Ibid.

18 Ibid.

19 Ibid.

20 Ibid.

21 GC Wenger, 'Nurturing Networks', *Demos Collection* 12 (1997).

22 Victor et al, *Loneliness, Social Isolation and Living Alone in Later Life*, ESRC Growing Older Programme, Research Findings 17.

23 See, for example, http://news.bbc.co.uk/1/hi/uk_politics/3652405.stm and http://society.guardian.co.uk/longtermcare/story/0,8150,1186111,00.html.

24 P Thane, '"I don't feel old": the experience of ageing in Britain, the last 175 years', the David Hobman Lecture, delivered at Kings College London, 26 Jan 2004, available at www.kcl.ac.uk/kis/schools/life_sciences/health/gerontology/docs/PatThane.pdf.

25 Victor et al, *Loneliness, Social Isolation and Living Alone in Later Life*, ESRC Growing Older Programme, Research Findings 17.

26 See T Bentley and J Wilsdon, 'Introduction' in T Bentley and J Wilsdon (eds), *The Adaptive State: strategies for personalising the public realm* (Demos, London, 2003).

27 B Schwartz, *The Paradox of Choice: why more is less* (New York: ECCO, 2004).

28 J Baldock and J Hadlow *Housebound Older People: the links between identity, self-esteem and the use of care services*, ESRC Growing Older Programme, Research Findings 4 (Sheffield: GOP, University of Sheffield, 2002).

29 Ibid.

30 Ibid.

31 Arber and Ginn, *Ageing and Gender*.

32 Victor et al, *Loneliness, Social Isolation and Living Alone in Later Life*, ESRC Growing Older Programme, Research Findings 17.

33 Great Britain. Department of Health, *Modernising Social Services: promoting independence, improving protection, raising standards*, Cm 4169 (London: The Stationery Office, 1998).

34 M Cattan, *Supporting Older People to Overcome Social Isolation and Loneliness* (Leeds Metropolitan University and Help the Aged, 2002).

35 A Osterle, 'Equity choices and long term care policies in Europe', in S Evans and G Clark, *The Care Crisis: an assessment of the crisis in Britain's care of the elderly* (London: Conservative Party Policy Unit, 2002).

36 ONS, *Social Trends* 34.
37 Ibid.
38 ONS, *Census 2001 National Report* (Titchfield: Office of National Statistics, 2003).
39 Arber and Ginn, *Ageing and Gender.*
40 See, for example, T Bignall and J Butt, *Between Ambition and Achievement: young black disabled people's views and experiences of independence and independent living* (Bristol: Policy Press for the Joseph Rowntree Foundation, 2000), available at www.jrf.org.uk/knowledge/findings/socialcare/340.asp.
41 Baldock and Hadlow, *Housebound Older People*, ESRC Growing Older Programme, Research Findings 4.
42 H McCarthy and P Miller, *London Calling: how mobile technologies can transform a city* (London: Demos, 2003) .
43 Cattan, *Supporting Older People to Overcome Social Isolation and Loneliness.*
44 T Scharf, C Phillipson, AE Smith and P Kingston, *Growing Older in Socially Deprived Areas: social exclusion in later life* (London: Help the Aged, 2002), available at: http://www.keele.ac.uk/depts/so/csg/ Growing_Older_in_Socially_Deprived_Areas_summary.pdf.
45 LGA, *All Our Tomorrows: inverting the triangle of care* (London: Local Government Association, 2002).
46 See Age Concern's response to *Equality and Diversity: Making it Happen* consultation paper, available at www.ageconcern.org.uk/AgeConcern/media/Ref2103AgeMatters.pdf.
47 Cited in LGA, *All Our Tomorrows.*
48 Ibid.
49 See Evans and Clark, *Care Crisis.*
50 J Huber and P Skidmore, *The New Old: why the baby boomers won't be pensioned off* (London: Demos, 2003).
51 See www.laingbuisson.co.uk/longtermcareconf.htm.
52 Royal Commission on Long Term Care, *With Respect to Old Age: long term care – rights and responsibilities,* a report by the Royal Commission on Long Term Care, Chairman: Professor Sir Stewart Sutherland, Cm 4192-I (London: Stationery Office, 1999).
53 Evans and Clark, *Care Crisis*, see table by Laing and Buisson.
54 *Independent Inquiry into Inequalities in Health*, chairman Sir Donald Acheson (London: Stationery Office, November 1998).
55 NAO, *Ensuring the Effective Discharge of Older Patients from NHS Acute Hospitals.*
56 See http://image.guardian.co.uk/sys-files/Society/documents/2003/02/17/ V07SMTV9.pdf.
57 Department of Health, *National Service Framework for Older People: executive summary* (London: Department of Health, 2001).
58 Ibid., Appendix 2.
59 LGA, *All Our Tomorrows.*
60 See www.adss.org.uk/committee/older/prevention.shtml.

61 LGA, *All Our Tomorrows*.

62 Department of Health, *National Service Framework for Older People: executive summary*.

63 See www.bhfactive.org.uk/areas_of_interest/afll/downloads/presentations/ MCFalls/FallsSummarySlides.pdf.

64 According to Age Concern, see www.ageconcern.org.uk/AgeConcern/1054_1158.htm.

65 See www.timebank.org.uk/aboutgiving/olderpeople.htm.

66 Strategy Unit, *Creating Public Value* (London: Strategy Unit, 2002).

67 Speech to the Guardian Public Services Summit, 29 Jan 2004.

68 T Bentley and J Wilsdon (eds), *The Adaptive State: strategies for personalising the public realm* (London: Demos, 2003).

69 Cattan, *Supporting Older People to Overcome Social Isolation and Loneliness*.

70 Ibid.

71 T Bentley, H McCarthy and M Mean, *Inside Out: rethinking inclusive communities* (London: Demos, 2003).

72 T Bentley and J Wilsdon, *The Adaptive State*; C Leadbeater, *Personalisation Through Participation* (London: Demos, 2004).

73 Leadbeater, *Personalisation Through Participation*.

74 J Hanson, 'Defining domesticity: housing and care choices for older people', the David Hobman lecture, delivered at Kings College London, 27 Jan 2003, available at www.kcl.ac.uk/kis/schools/life_sciences/health/gerontology/ Annual_files/frame.htm.

75 D Gann, J Barlow and T Venables, *Digital Futures: making homes smarter* (Coventry: Chartered Institute of Housing, 1999).

76 T Bignall and J Butt (2001) *Between Ambition and Achievement: young black disabled people's views and experiences of independence and independent living* (Bristol: Policy Press, 2001).

77 R Hummer et al, 'Religious involvement and US adult mortality', *Demography* 36, no 2 (1999), and J Rietschlin 'Voluntary association membership and psychological distress', *Journal of Health and Social Behaviour* 39 (1998).

78 Cattan, *Supporting Older People to Overcome Social Isolation and Loneliness*.

79 See www.ageconcern.org.uk/AgeConcern/staying.htm.

80 See www.communitytransport.com/.

81 See www.ectgroup.co.uk/.

82 Cabinet Office. Performance and Inovation Unit. *Winning the Generation Game: improving opportunities for people aged 50–65 in work and community activity* (London: Stationery Office, 2000).

83 Scharf et al, *Growing Older in Socially Deprived Areas*.

84 ONS *Social Trends* 32 (2002), available at www.csv-rsvp.org.uk/ history.htm.

85 *Health Survey for England 2000: the health of older people* (London: Stationery Office), available at www.official-documents.co.uk/document/deps/doh/ survey00/summ.htm.

86   See, for example, M Riseborough and C Jenkins, *Now You See Me…Now You Don't: how are older citizens being included in regeneration?* (London: Age Concern, 2004).

87   Social Exclusion Unit, *Making the Connections: final report on transport and social exclusion* (London: Social Exclusion Unit, 2003).

DEMOS – Licence to Publish

THE WORK (AS DEFINED BELOW) IS PROVIDED UNDER THE TERMS OF THIS LICENCE ("LICENCE"). THE WORK IS PROTECTED BY COPYRIGHT AND/OR OTHER APPLICABLE LAW. ANY USE OF THE WORK OTHER THAN AS AUTHORIZED UNDER THIS LICENCE IS PROHIBITED. BY EXERCISING ANY RIGHTS TO THE WORK PROVIDED HERE, YOU ACCEPT AND AGREE TO BE BOUND BY THE TERMS OF THIS LICENCE. DEMOS GRANTS YOU THE RIGHTS CONTAINED HERE IN CONSIDERATION OF YOUR ACCEPTANCE OF SUCH TERMS AND CONDITIONS.

1. **Definitions**
   a **"Collective Work"** means a work, such as a periodical issue, anthology or encyclopedia, in which the Work in its entirety in unmodified form, along with a number of other contributions, constituting separate and independent works in themselves, are assembled into a collective whole. A work that constitutes a Collective Work will not be considered a Derivative Work (as defined below) for the purposes of this Licence.
   b **"Derivative Work"** means a work based upon the Work or upon the Work and other pre-existing works, such as a musical arrangement, dramatization, fictionalization, motion picture version, sound recording, art reproduction, abridgment, condensation, or any other form in which the Work may be recast, transformed, or adapted, except that a work that constitutes a Collective Work or a translation from English into another language will not be considered a Derivative Work for the purpose of this Licence.
   c **"Licensor"** means the individual or entity that offers the Work under the terms of this Licence.
   d **"Original Author"** means the individual or entity who created the Work.
   e **"Work"** means the copyrightable work of authorship offered under the terms of this Licence.
   f **"You"** means an individual or entity exercising rights under this Licence who has not previously violated the terms of this Licence with respect to the Work, or who has received express permission from DEMOS to exercise rights under this Licence despite a previous violation.
2. **Fair Use Rights.** Nothing in this licence is intended to reduce, limit, or restrict any rights arising from fair use, first sale or other limitations on the exclusive rights of the copyright owner under copyright law or other applicable laws.
3. **Licence Grant.** Subject to the terms and conditions of this Licence, Licensor hereby grants You a worldwide, royalty-free, non-exclusive, perpetual (for the duration of the applicable copyright) licence to exercise the rights in the Work as stated below:
   a to reproduce the Work, to incorporate the Work into one or more Collective Works, and to reproduce the Work as incorporated in the Collective Works;
   b to distribute copies or phonorecords of, display publicly, perform publicly, and perform publicly by means of a digital audio transmission the Work including as incorporated in Collective Works;
   The above rights may be exercised in all media and formats whether now known or hereafter devised. The above rights include the right to make such modifications as are technically necessary to exercise the rights in other media and formats. All rights not expressly granted by Licensor are hereby reserved.
4. **Restrictions.** The licence granted in Section 3 above is expressly made subject to and limited by the following restrictions:
   a You may distribute, publicly display, publicly perform, or publicly digitally perform the Work only under the terms of this Licence, and You must include a copy of, or the Uniform Resource Identifier for, this Licence with every copy or phonorecord of the Work You distribute, publicly display, publicly perform, or publicly digitally perform. You may not offer or impose any terms on the Work that alter or restrict the terms of this Licence or the recipients' exercise of the rights granted hereunder. You may not sublicence the Work. You must keep intact all notices that refer to this Licence and to the disclaimer of warranties. You may not distribute, publicly display, publicly perform, or publicly digitally perform the Work with any technological measures that control access or use of the Work in a manner inconsistent with the terms of this Licence Agreement. The above applies to the Work as incorporated in a Collective Work, but this does not require the Collective Work apart from the Work itself to be made subject to the terms of this Licence. If You create a Collective Work, upon notice from any Licencor You must, to the extent practicable, remove from the Collective Work any reference to such Licensor or the Original Author, as requested.
   b You may not exercise any of the rights granted to You in Section 3 above in any manner that is primarily intended for or directed toward commercial advantage or private monetary

compensation. The exchange of the Work for other copyrighted works by means of digital file-sharing or otherwise shall not be considered to be intended for or directed toward commercial advantage or private monetary compensation, provided there is no payment of any monetary compensation in connection with the exchange of copyrighted works.

c If you distribute, publicly display, publicly perform, or publicly digitally perform the Work or any Collective Works, You must keep intact all copyright notices for the Work and give the Original Author credit reasonable to the medium or means You are utilizing by conveying the name (or pseudonym if applicable) of the Original Author if supplied; the title of the Work if supplied. Such credit may be implemented in any reasonable manner; provided, however, that in the case of a Collective Work, at a minimum such credit will appear where any other comparable authorship credit appears and in a manner at least as prominent as such other comparable authorship credit.

5. Representations, Warranties and Disclaimer

a By offering the Work for public release under this Licence, Licensor represents and warrants that, to the best of Licensor's knowledge after reasonable inquiry:

i Licensor has secured all rights in the Work necessary to grant the licence rights hereunder and to permit the lawful exercise of the rights granted hereunder without You having any obligation to pay any royalties, compulsory licence fees, residuals or any other payments;

ii The Work does not infringe the copyright, trademark, publicity rights, common law rights or any other right of any third party or constitute defamation, invasion of privacy or other tortious injury to any third party.

b EXCEPT AS EXPRESSLY STATED IN THIS LICENCE OR OTHERWISE AGREED IN WRITING OR REQUIRED BY APPLICABLE LAW, THE WORK IS LICENCED ON AN "AS IS" BASIS, WITHOUT WARRANTIES OF ANY KIND, EITHER EXPRESS OR IMPLIED INCLUDING, WITHOUT LIMITATION, ANY WARRANTIES REGARDING THE CONTENTS OR ACCURACY OF THE WORK.

6. Limitation on Liability. EXCEPT TO THE EXTENT REQUIRED BY APPLICABLE LAW, AND EXCEPT FOR DAMAGES ARISING FROM LIABILITY TO A THIRD PARTY RESULTING FROM BREACH OF THE WARRANTIES IN SECTION 5, IN NO EVENT WILL LICENSOR BE LIABLE TO YOU ON ANY LEGAL THEORY FOR ANY SPECIAL, INCIDENTAL, CONSEQUENTIAL, PUNITIVE OR EXEMPLARY DAMAGES ARISING OUT OF THIS LICENCE OR THE USE OF THE WORK, EVEN IF LICENSOR HAS BEEN ADVISED OF THE POSSIBILITY OF SUCH DAMAGES.

7. Termination

a This Licence and the rights granted hereunder will terminate automatically upon any breach by You of the terms of this Licence. Individuals or entities who have received Collective Works from You under this Licence, however, will not have their licences terminated provided such individuals or entities remain in full compliance with those licences. Sections 1, 2, 5, 6, 7, and 8 will survive any termination of this Licence.

b Subject to the above terms and conditions, the licence granted here is perpetual (for the duration of the applicable copyright in the Work). Notwithstanding the above, Licensor reserves the right to release the Work under different licence terms or to stop distributing the Work at any time; provided, however that any such election will not serve to withdraw this Licence (or any other licence that has been, or is required to be, granted under the terms of this Licence), and this Licence will continue in full force and effect unless terminated as stated above.

8. Miscellaneous

a Each time You distribute or publicly digitally perform the Work or a Collective Work, DEMOS offers to the recipient a licence to the Work on the same terms and conditions as the licence granted to You under this Licence.

b If any provision of this Licence is invalid or unenforceable under applicable law, it shall not affect the validity or enforceability of the remainder of the terms of this Licence, and without further action by the parties to this agreement, such provision shall be reformed to the minimum extent necessary to make such provision valid and enforceable.

c No term or provision of this Licence shall be deemed waived and no breach consented to unless such waiver or consent shall be in writing and signed by the party to be charged with such waiver or consent.

d This Licence constitutes the entire agreement between the parties with respect to the Work licensed here. There are no understandings, agreements or representations with respect to the Work not specified here. Licensor shall not be bound by any additional provisions that may appear in any communication from You. This Licence may not be modified without the mutual written agreement of DEMOS and You.